DRAW

PORTRAITS
AND THE
HUMAN FIGURE

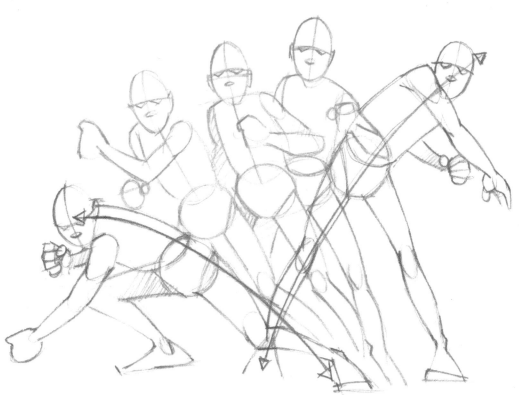

BOOK  HOUSE

Contents

SALARIYA

Published in Great Britain in MMXIII by
Book House, an imprint of
The Salariya Book Company Ltd
25 Marlborough Place, Brighton BN1 1UB

1 3 5 7 9 8 6 4 2

Please visit our website at **www.salariya.com**
for **free** electronic versions of:
You Wouldn't Want to Be an Egyptian Mummy!
You Wouldn't Want to Be a Roman Gladiator!
You Wouldn't Want to be a Polar Explorer!
You Wouldn't Want to sail on a 19th-Century Whaling Ship!

Authors:
Mark Bergin was born in Hastings in 1961.
He studied at Eastbourne College of Art and has
specialised in historical reconstructions as well as aviation
and maritime subjects since 1983. He lives in
Bexhill-on-Sea with his wife and three children.

David Antram was born in Brighton, England, in 1958.
He studied at Eastbourne College of Art and then worked in
advertising for fifteen years before becoming a full-time artist.
He has illustrated many children's non-fiction books.

Editor: Rob Walker

PB ISBN: 978-1-908759-66-5

A CIP catalogue record for this
book is available from the
British Library.

Printed and bound in China.
Printed on paper from
sustainable sources.

PAPER FROM
SUSTAINABLE
FORESTS

**WARNING: Fixatives should be
used only under adult supervision.**

FIND OUR BOOKS
ON THE APP STORE:
SEARCH FOR 'SALARIYA'

@bookhousebooks   The Salariya   BookHouse100
                  Book Company

Visit our **new** online shop at
shop.salariya.com
for special offers, gift ideas, all our new releases
and free postage and packaging.

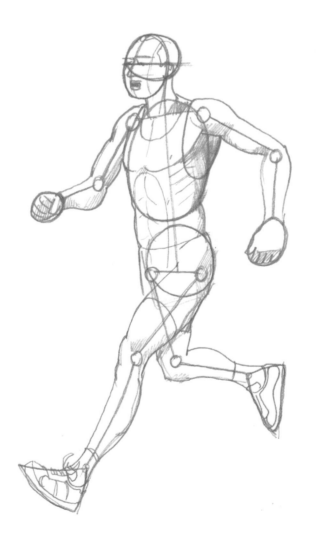

Making a start
DRAW

Learning to draw is about looking and seeing. Keep practising, and get to know your subject. Use a sketchbook to make quick drawings. Start by doodling, and experiment with shapes and patterns. There are many ways to draw; this book shows only some methods. Visit art galleries, look at artists' drawings, see how friends draw, but above all, find your own way.

You can practise drawing figures using an artist's wooden model to try out various poses.

When drawing from photos, use construction lines to help you to understand the form of the body and the relationship between each of its parts.

Sketch people in everyday surroundings. This will help you to draw faster to capture the main elements of a pose quickly.

Try sketching friends and family at home.

You can create new poses by drawing simple stick figures.

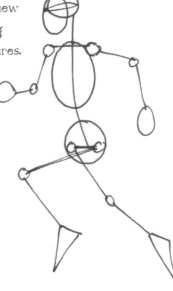

Drawing materials

Try using different types of drawing paper and materials. Experiment with charcoal, wax crayons and pastels. All pens, from felt-tips to ballpoints, will make interesting marks — you could also try drawing with pen and ink on wet paper.

Pencil

Felt-tip

Hard **pencils** are greyer and soft pencils are blacker. Hard pencils are graded from 6H (the hardest) through 5H, 4H, 3H and 2H to H. Soft pencils are graded from B, 2B, 3B, 4B and 5B up to 6B (the softest).

Silhouette is a style of drawing that mainly uses only solid black shapes.

Lines drawn in **ink** cannot be erased, so keep your ink drawings sketchy and less rigid. Don't worry about mistakes as these lines can be lost in the drawing as it develops.

Ink

Charcoal is very soft and can be used for big, bold drawings. Ask an adult to spray your charcoal drawing with fixative to prevent it smudging.

You can create special effects by scraping away parts of a drawing done with **wax crayons.**

Pastels are even softer than charcoal, and come in a wide range of colours. Ask an adult to spray your pastel drawing with fixative to prevent it smudging.

9

Perspective

DRAW

If you look at a figure from different viewpoints, you will see that whichever part is closest to you looks larger, and the part furthest away from you looks smallest. Drawing in perspective is a way of creating a feeling of depth – of suggesting three dimensions on a flat surface.

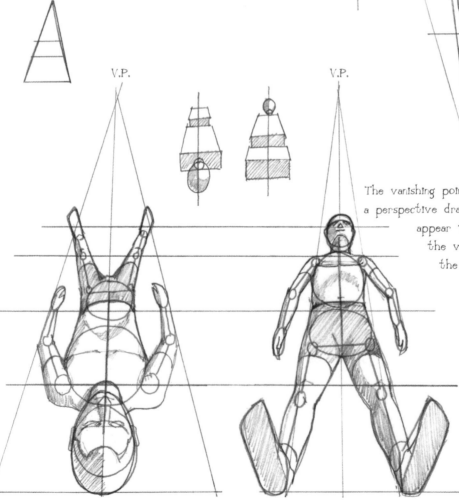

V.P.

V.P.

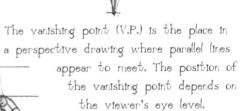

The vanishing point (V.P.) is the place in a perspective drawing where parallel lines appear to meet. The position of the vanishing point depends on the viewer's eye level.

Two-point perspective drawing

Two-point perspective uses two vanishing points: one for lines running along the length of the object, and another on the opposite side for lines running across the width of the object.

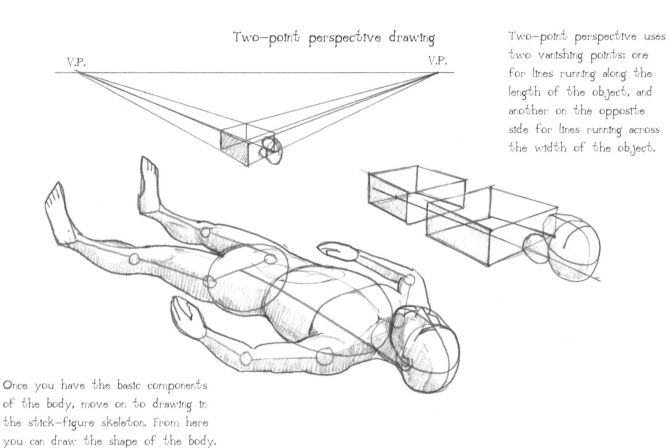

Once you have the basic components of the body, move on to drawing in the stick-figure skeleton. From here you can draw the shape of the body.

Three-point perspective drawing

Three-point perspective drawings use three vanishing points. This method is good for drawing objects at angles.

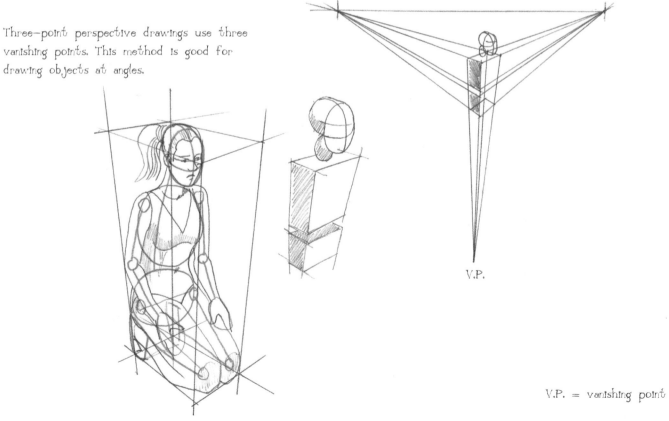

V.P. = vanishing point

11

Figure proportions

T his page shows the standard proportions of a human figure. Normally the length of a human head will fit seven or eight times into its body height.

The proportions of a male figure shown from different views.

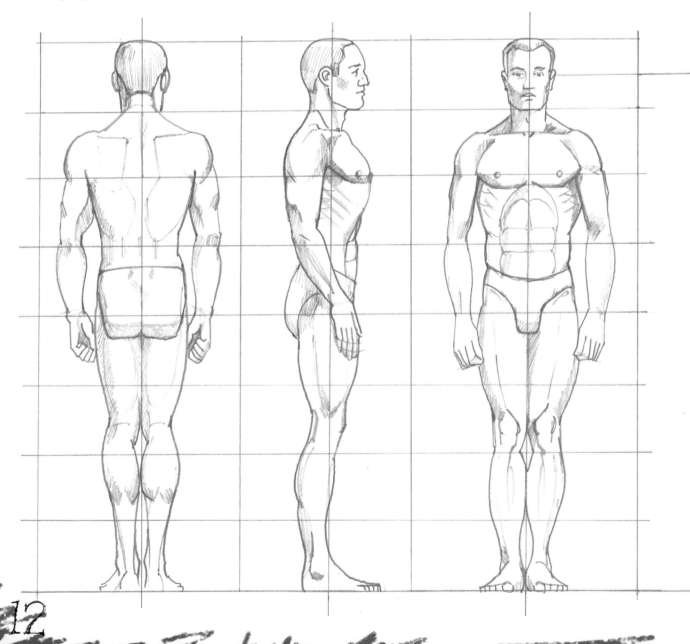

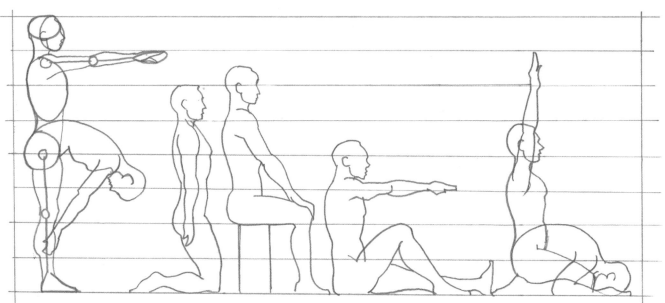

This shows the height variation of a figure in different positions.

The proportions of a female figure shown from different views.

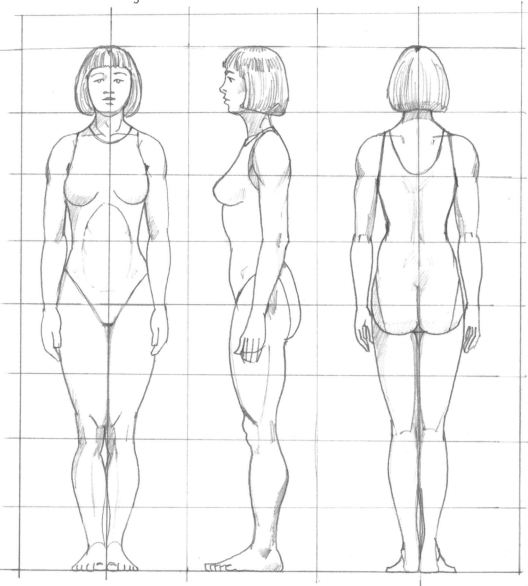

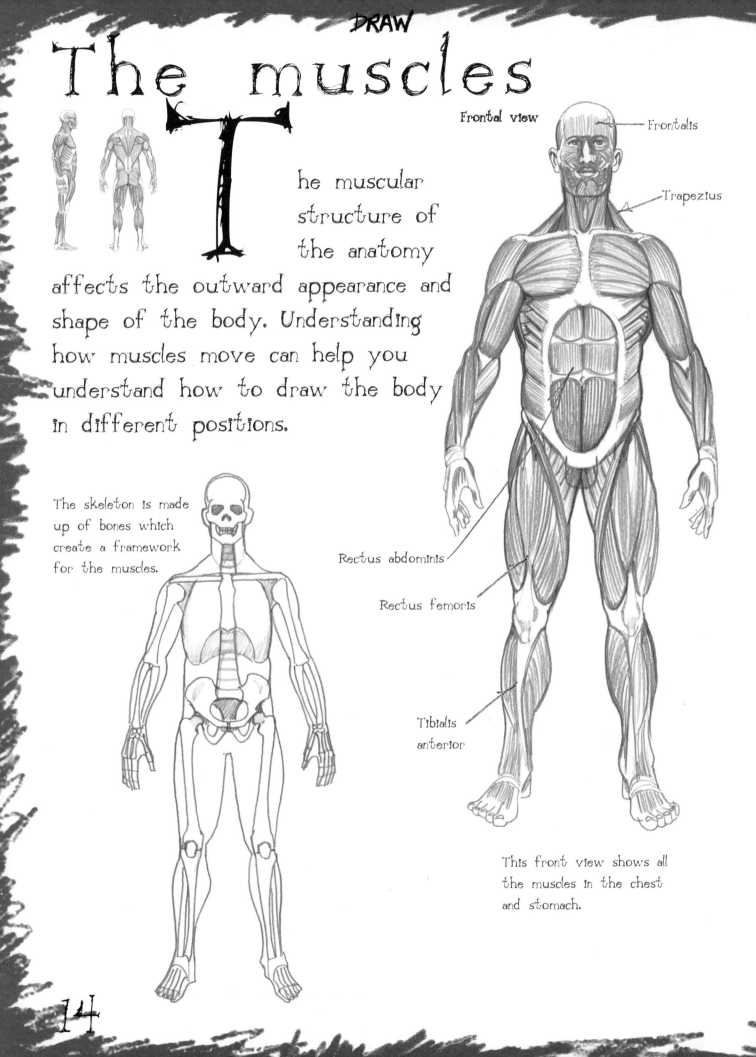

The muscles

The muscular structure of the anatomy affects the outward appearance and shape of the body. Understanding how muscles move can help you understand how to draw the body in different positions.

Frontal view

Frontalis

Trapezius

The skeleton is made up of bones which create a framework for the muscles.

Rectus abdominis

Rectus femoris

Tibialis anterior

This front view shows all the muscles in the chest and stomach.

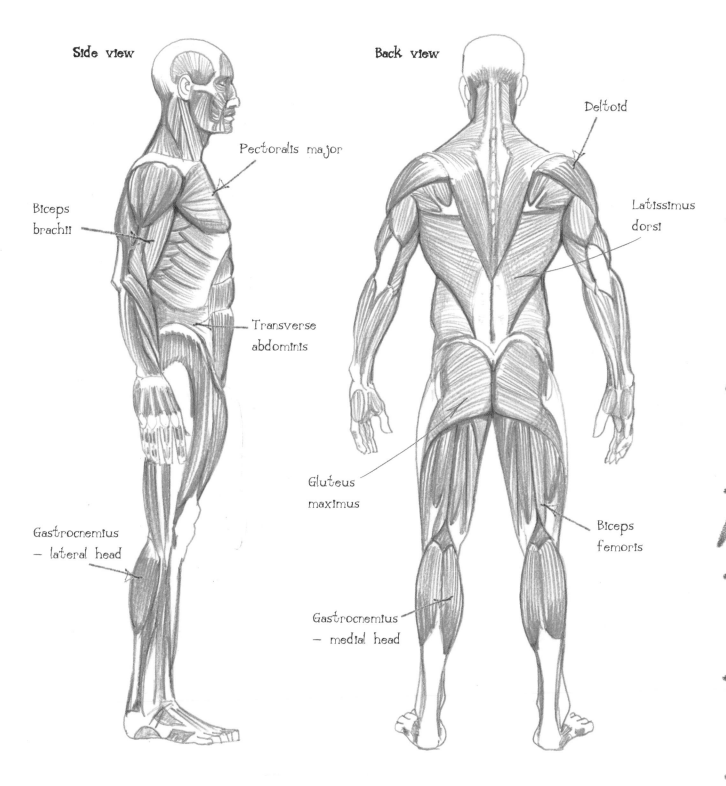

Side view

Pectoralis major

Biceps
brachii

Transverse
abdominis

Gastrocnemius
– lateral head

Back view

Deltoid

Latissimus
dorsi

Gluteus
maximus

Biceps
femoris

Gastrocnemius
– medial head

This view shows all the muscular
structure from the side.

This view shows all the muscular
structure from the back.

Bones and muscles

A little understanding of the shape of the skull and the muscle structure that lies under the skin can really help when drawing the human head. The outward apperance of a human head is based entirely on the underlying shape of the hard bone and muscle contours.

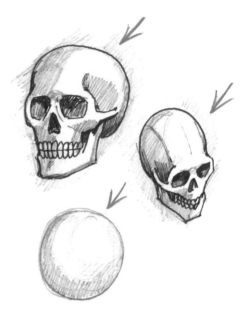

Here we can see the effect of a light source on the skull. Note which areas become darker as the skull changes position.

These two drawings are of the skull from a side view and a frontal view.

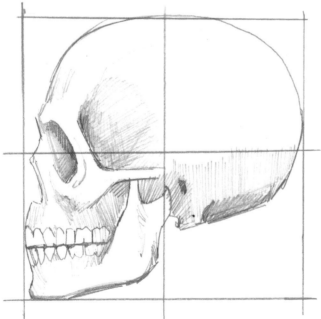

Using a grid helps you to keep the skull in proportion.

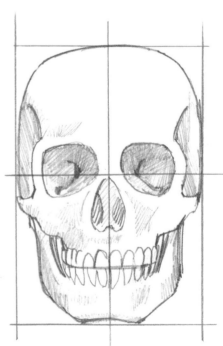

Dividing your drawing into four sections for a frontal view can help you maintain the symmetry of the skull.

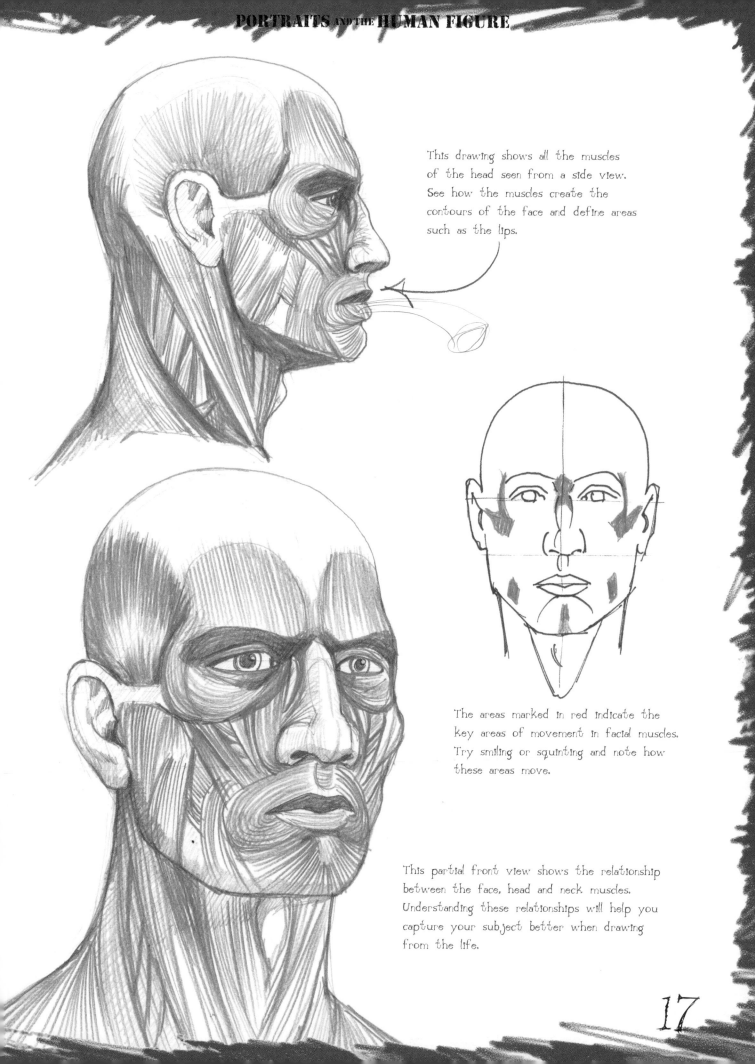

This drawing shows all the muscles of the head seen from a side view. See how the muscles create the contours of the face and define areas such as the lips.

The areas marked in red indicate the key areas of movement in facial muscles. Try smiling or squinting and note how these areas move.

This partial front view shows the relationship between the face, head and neck muscles. Understanding these relationships will help you capture your subject better when drawing from the life.

17

The head

DRAW

Heads are difficult shapes to draw. The face includes some of the most expressive features of the body. Using construction lines helps to place the eyes, nose, ears and mouth accurately on the head.

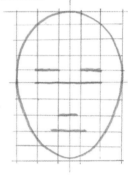

Frontal view

Squaring up the paper can help you with the positioning of the facial features.

Establish the main shape of the head by overlapping two ovals.

Construction lines help you to keep the features in the correct positions when drawing the head from different angles.

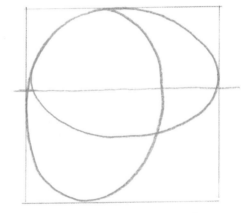

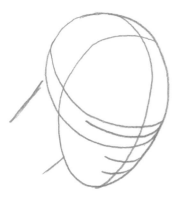

Draw construction lines to indicate the position of each facial feature.

These construction lines have been used to draw a male head.

These construction lines have been used to draw a female head.

Use downward curving construction lines to show the head looking downwards.

Accurate construction lines make it much easier to draw in the facial features and details.

Use upward curving construction lines to show the head looking up.

Draw in the features. Do not forget the underside of the chin.

Complete any details and remove unwanted construction lines.

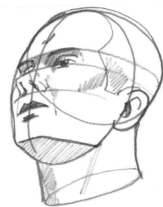

19

The eyes

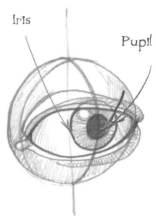

Iris

Pupil

Each eyeball sits in a socket in the head. It is surrounded by the protective eyelids. The eyes and eyebrows are very expressive.

The eyeball is spherical in shape. Its most visible features are the iris and pupil. Start by drawing a spherical eyeball. Add the shape of the eyelids.

Male eye

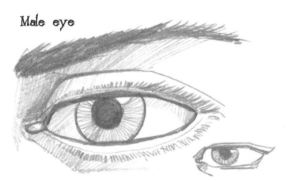

Once the visible part of the eye is drawn add detail to the iris. Leave an area of white for a highlight.

Female eye

Consider details around the eye; the length of the eyelashes and the eyebrow shape.

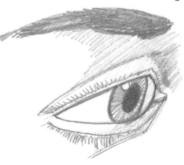

When drawing the eye from the side it is important to use perspective.

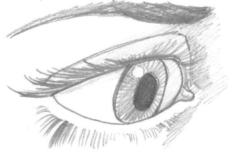

Check your light source before adding tone to the drawing. Darker areas tend to be where the nose projects out from the eyes.

Eyes from below

Eyes from above

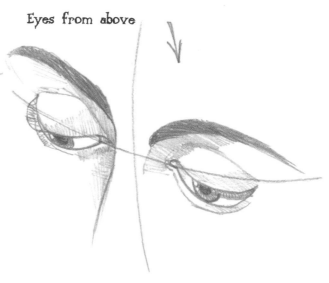

When drawing the eyes from this angle, use a downward-curved construction line to place them accurately.

Drawing the eyes from above means you see less of the eyeball.

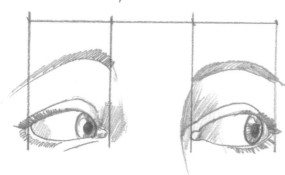

When drawing both eyes it is very important that they relate correctly in scale. It helps to start your drawing using carefully worked out construction lines.

With this view it is important to consider the light source.

Partially shut eyelids show less of the eyeball. Add more shaded areas.

The position of the pupil and iris is important as it shows where the eyes are looking. Keep their direction similar.

The mouth DRAW

The mouth is very expressive and can give an insight into a person's mood or their emotions.

These are the basic construction lines for drawing lips from the side.

Once the construction lines are in place use them as a guide to create the tone of the lips.

Upward curving construction lines are used to draw the mouth from below.

Construction lines for a front view.

When adding tone to the lips always use lines curving into the mouth to create shape. Add more lines where more shade is needed.

Mouths can be very expressive. Practise drawing your own mouth from a variety of different angles.

Here the mouth is seen slightly open.

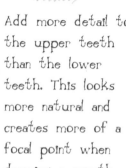

Add more detail to the upper teeth than the lower teeth. This looks more natural and creates more of a focal point when drawing a mouth.

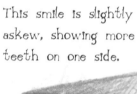

Side view of mouth, biting the bottom lip.

This smile is slightly askew, showing more teeth on one side.

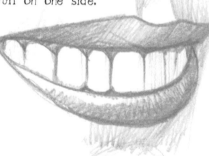

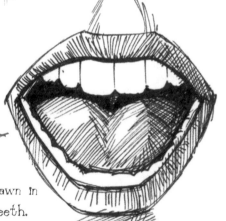

This open mouth, drawn in pen, shows all the teeth.

This mouth is open but the lips hide the teeth.

This looks like a happy expressive smile.

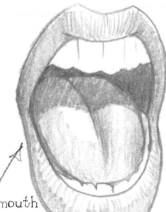

This wide open mouth is probably shouting.

23

Noses

This shows the basic areas of shading needed to give a nose its shape.

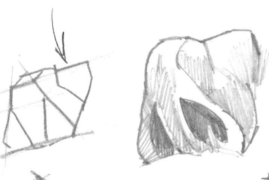

oses come in a vast variety of shapes and sizes. Drawing a nose from different angles is a key skill to learn when drawing the head.

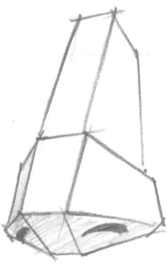

These construction lines help you to draw the nose from below.

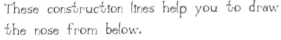

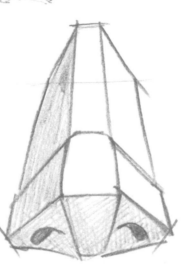

The darkest area of the nose is inside the nostril.

These three sets of construction lines show the shape of the nose from different angles. Use this basic shape to create the nose in all shapes and sizes.

Adding tone to the nose is very important because it creates and emphasises its shape. Study the nose to see how the light hits it and add tone to clarify its shape and angle.

Noses differ greatly. Pay attention to any kinks and bumps which make a nose individual.

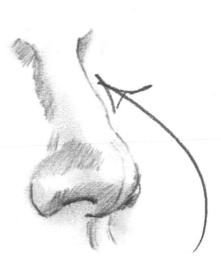

Use highlights where appropriate.

Always relate the nose to the other facial features to get the proportions right.

Ears

The variation in people's ears is endless, as no two ears are the same, even on the same head. An ear is quite a complicated form and is drawn almost entirely using curved lines.

Draw the basic shape of the ear with one curved line.

Draw curved lines to create the structure.

Add tone to create a three-dimensional feel to the ear structure.

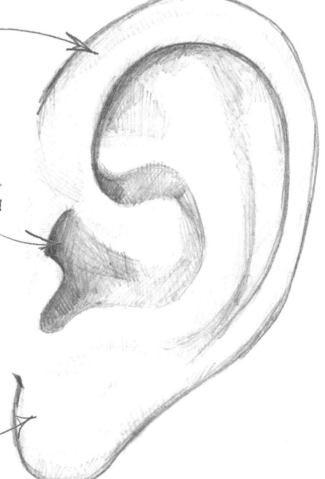

Add shading to the ear hole and its complicated folds where less light reaches.

The earlobe usually catches most of the light.

The ear comes in so many shapes and sizes. Look carefully at them when drawing a subject as the shape may be quite distinctive.

This ear has quite a rounded shape.

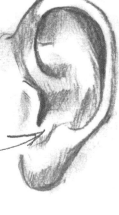

Earlobes come in many shapes and sizes. Some extend below the ear while others attach directly to the head.

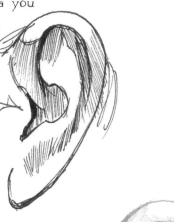

Some ears have tighter curves which creates more shadow.

Ears can look very different depending on what media you draw them in.

Use construction lines to help you to form the shape of the ear. Remove them when you are finished.

Remember the ear will cast a shadow depending on the direction of the light source.

27

Light sources

DRAW

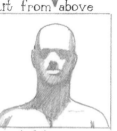

The light source for a drawing can have a huge effect on the finished picture. Placing your model beside a well-lit window or another strong light source will give you stark contrasts to create a dynamic image.

Lit from above

From the side

No lighting

From below

The effect of different light sources.

The face is drawn with its light source from the right, casting the left side of the face into shadow.

← Light source.

This drawing is done in white chalk on black paper. Use highlights instead of shading to create the shape of the face. Note exactly how the light source hits the subject.

Light source

Use the negative effect of drawing with a light material on dark paper to give your drawing added drama.

Light source

Light source

Light source

Light source

When light hits a domed surface, shading must be applied gradually from light to dark.

29

Young people

Drawing a child's head is very different from drawing an adult head. The proportions of the face and head change quite considerably.

Draw two overlapping ovals for the shape of the head.

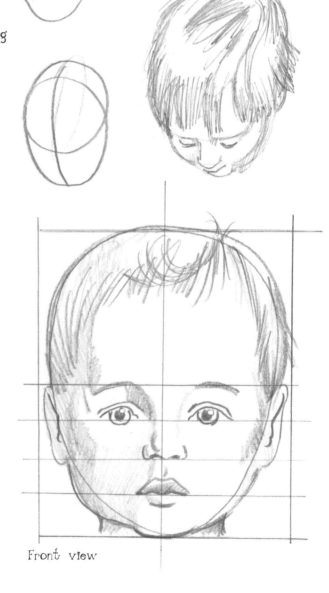

Construction lines help you to measure the head's features and proportions.

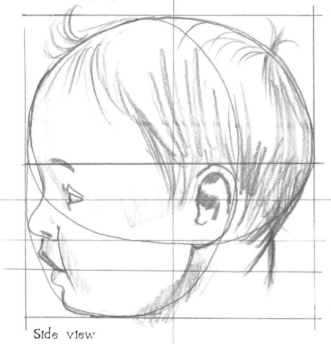

Side view

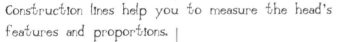

Front view

Use construction lines to help proportion and position features.

Practise drawing children's heads in many different positions.

Draw in the hair shape using simple, flowing lines.

Sketch in the facial features and other details.

Ink line drawings can be very effective. Keep the lines simple — do not overwork or you will age the features.

A sleeping child is a great subject to draw.

31

DRAW
The elderly

As people age their facial features become more exaggerated and distinct. The face gradually acquires folds, wrinkles and lines. This can make a person fascinating to draw.

This brow shows many wrinkles and lines; details which define an elderly person's portrait.

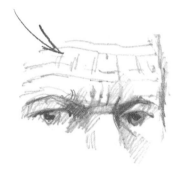

Note the detail around the eye. 'Crows' feet' spread from the outer corners of each eye.

Add more lines around the mouth to suggest wrinkles.

Add curved lines under the chin and around the throat to show the effect of aging skin.

Lines around the nose are more pronounced than on a younger person.

This simple ink line drawing uses no tone but still suggests age through its careful use of curved lines.

When drawing someone who is balding, study the shape of the hairline carefully.

This portrait relies on heavy patched tone to convey the age of the subject.

In old age the structure of the face becomes more delineated but colour fades. Eyebrows, hair and lips become less defined.

33

Expressions

Facial expressions can convey an enormous insight into a person's emotions or reactions.

Try looking at your drawing in a mirror. Seeing it in reverse can help you spot mistakes.

These small thumbnail sketches show a simple guide to everyday facial expressions.

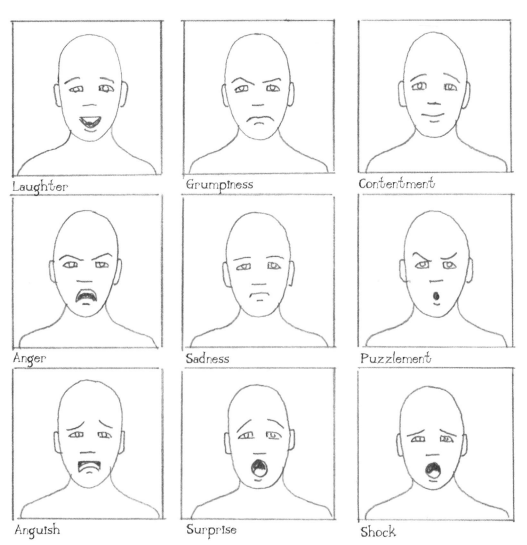

Laughter

Grumpiness

Contentment

Anger

Sadness

Puzzlement

Anguish

Surprise

Shock

Always start your drawing of a head with two overlapping ovals to get the shape right.

Refer to the simple guides to help you create the expression you want. Then build up the features and add details.

Use construction lines to proportion your portrait.

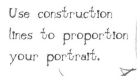

Note that certain expressions can wrinkle the skin, causing temporary lines.

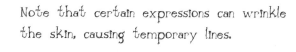

Draw Self-portraits

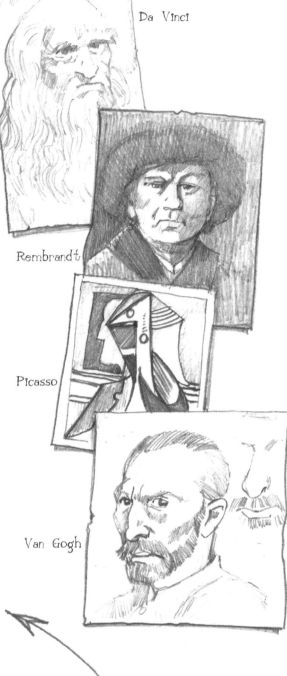

Da Vinci

Rembrandt

Picasso

Van Gogh

Self-portraits have been done throughout the history of art. Great artists such as Da Vinci, Rembrandt, Picasso and Van Gogh have all left impressions of themselves in drawings and paintings.

Light source

Draw yourself in a mirror to practise drawing portraits. Use a good light source such as a window and remember that your drawing will be in reverse.

Try concentrating on particular details of your face, like the eye or nose for example. These could the be arranged together to form an interesting composition.

Create an interesting line drawing. Study a photograph of yourself and try to recognise your most defining features. Now trace the photograph and try to capture your likeness with as few lines as possible.

Create an unusual, dynamic portrait. Draw a silhouette of your profile. Combine it with half of a front view self-portrait.

37

DRAW
Accessories

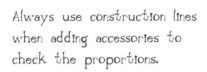

Hats, glasses and facial hair can all stamp personality on a subject. Each can give a valuable insight into what defines a person's identity.

Always use construction lines when adding accessories to check the proportions.

When adding glasses, take care to position them correctly on the nose and ears.

Always check the negative space — the area around your drawing. This can help you spot mistakes.

Take care to get the overall shape of the beard correct. Draw in lots of short lines to show the direction of the hairs.

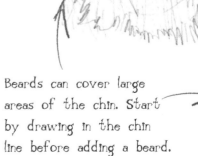

Beards can cover large areas of the chin. Start by drawing in the chin line before adding a beard.

Hats come in many shapes and sizes, and sit on the head in different ways.

Draw circular construction lines to position the hat correctly on the head.

Consider the width and height of the hat and make sure it fits around the head.

Remember that a hat brim will cast a shadow over the face.

Hats can be worn at all angles, which can help you to capture a person's character.

Caps sit very tight on the head and only cast a shadow on the front of the face.

39

DRAW The hands

The hand is one of the most complex parts of a figure to draw. It consists of many moving parts, and therefore can be drawn in a huge variety of poses.

The hand can be broken down into basic shapes and areas.

Each finger has three sections, a thumb has two sections, and the main area of the hand has three.

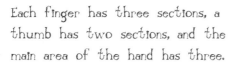

Sketch in these shapes as three-dimensional boxes. Construction lines can then be drawn for a variety of poses.

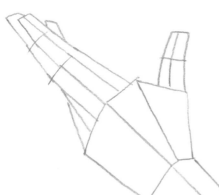

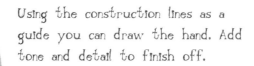

Using the construction lines as a guide you can draw the hand. Add tone and detail to finish off.

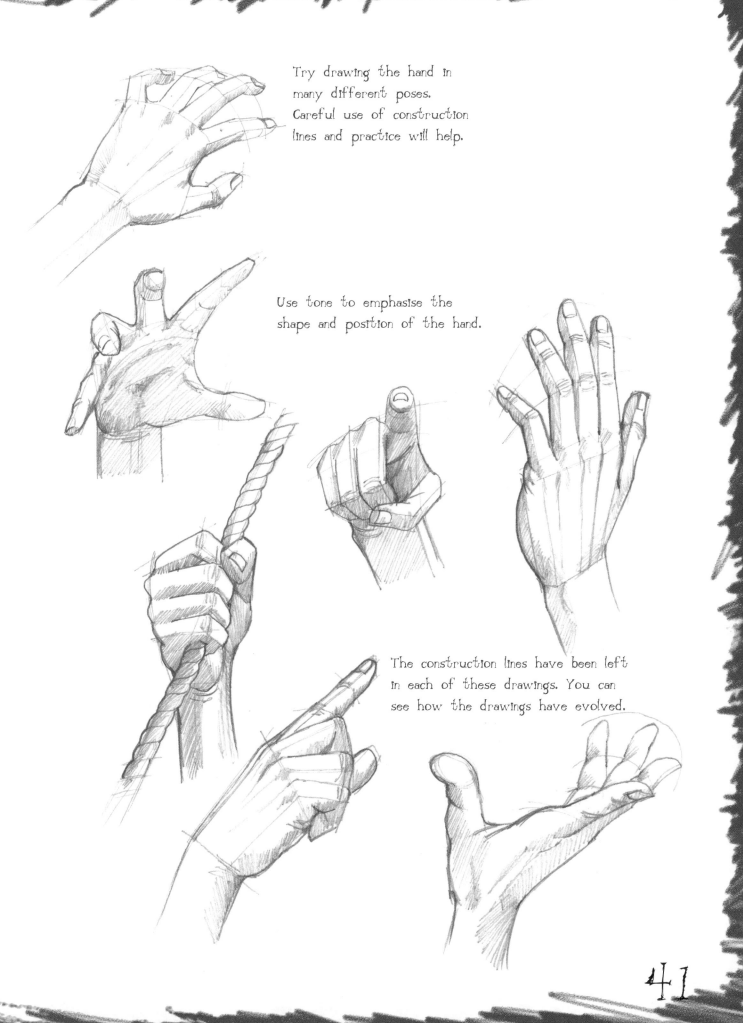

Try drawing the hand in
many different poses.
Careful use of construction
lines and practice will help.

Use tone to emphasise the
shape and position of the hand.

The construction lines have been left
in each of these drawings. You can
see how the drawings have evolved.

The Feet
DRAW

Feet come in all shapes and sizes and can be drawn in many different poses. The construction lines for a simple side view usually start with a triangle shape, then the toes are added and the ankle is positioned.

The shape of the foot can be broken down into simple three-dimensional shapes.

Using these construction lines as a guide, draw in the toes and anklebone.

A simple triangular-shaped side view of the foot.

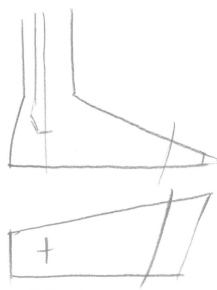

The base of the foot is a simple trapezoid shape. Indicate the toes and the ball of the foot.

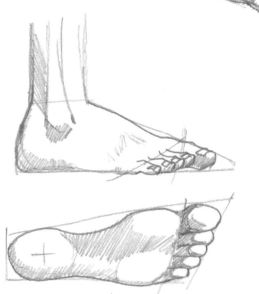

Using these construction lines as a guide, draw in both views of the foot.

This page shows the foot drawn in a variety of different poses. The construction lines have been left in to show how the shape and position of the foot have evolved.

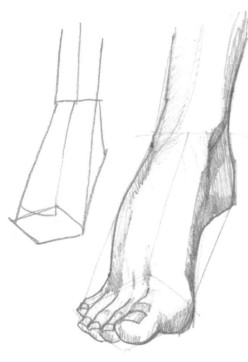

Draw in the toes. Position them within the area of the construction lines.

Add tone to your drawing to indicate the direction of the light source.

43

Standing figure

A standing figure can be drawn using a simple framework of construction lines. This basic starting point is a very good way to establish the correct proportions of a human figure in your drawing. The standing figure is a surfer holding his board.

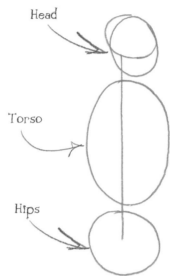

Head

Torso

Hips

Start by drawing in a large oval between two circles for the head, torso and hips; Add a centre line.

Add two small circles for the shoulders either side of the large oval.

Draw two small circles either side of the hips; this will be the top of the legs. Draw a horizontal line to join the circles.

Draw in both arms using straight lines. Indicate the elbow joints using straight lines.

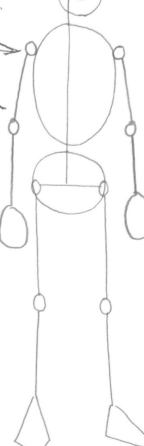

Add ovals to each arm for the hands

Add straight lines for both legs. Indicate the knee joints with small circles.

Add triangles to show the shape and direction of the feet.

44

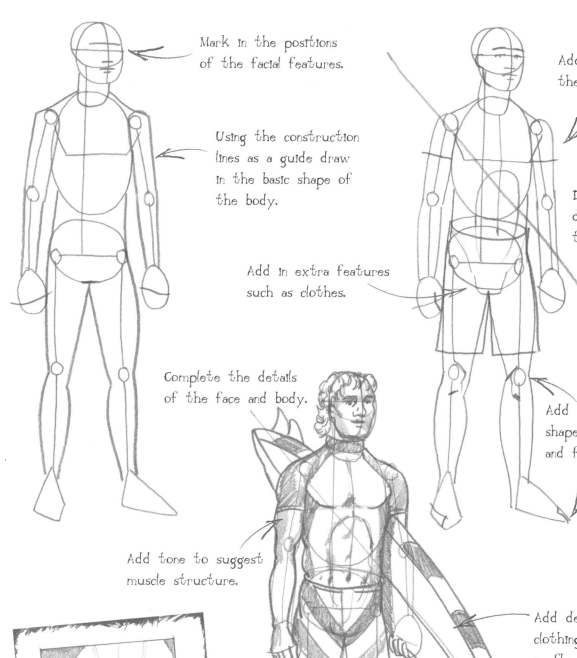

Mark in the positions of the facial features.

Using the construction lines as a guide draw in the basic shape of the body.

Add more detail to the face and torso.

Draw in a diagonal line for the surfboard.

Add in extra features such as clothes.

Add details to the shape of the knees and feet.

Complete the details of the face and body.

Add tone to suggest muscle structure.

Add detail to clothing and surfboard.

Look at the shapes in between the lines of your drawing (known as negative space). This can help you spot mistakes.

Draw in hands.

Shade in areas where light would not reach.

Remove any unwanted construction lines.

45

Balance and motion

DRAW

Motion and balance are important aspects to consider in your drawing. Use basic construction lines to create a variety of poses. Then build up the drawing from there.

A ballet dancer is a perfect example to show balance in the human body.

Draw in the position of the head and body using construction lines (as shown in previous pages). Pay particular attention to the curve and direction of the spine and hips.

Add the limbs; indicate the elbow and knee joints with small circles between straight lines. Draw in the hand positions using ovals and draw triangles for each foot.

Using construction lines draw a simple stick figure either running or walking. Study people as they walk by to see how their body moves.

A tennis player. Note the changes in balance as the racket is swung.

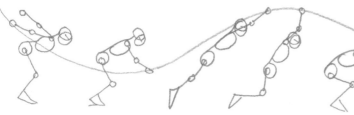

This figure is performing a long jump. The red line shows the flow of the hands through each stage of the jump.

When the basic structure of the figure is complete, start building up the shape of the body.

Keep the drawing quite light and sketchy at first until you are confident that the proportions are right.

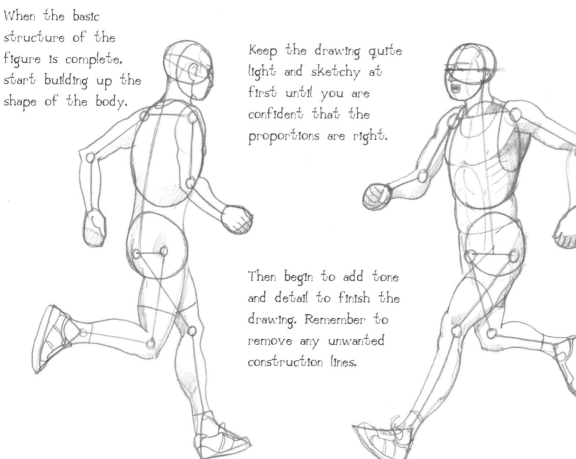

Then begin to add tone and detail to finish the drawing. Remember to remove any unwanted construction lines.

47

Walking DRAW figure

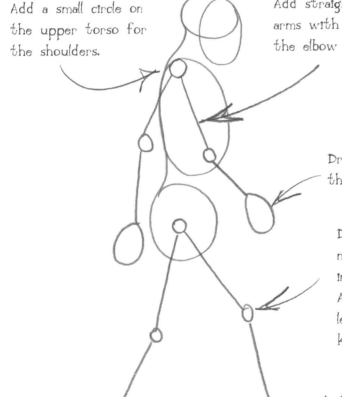

A simple walking movement is a good starting point for drawing a figure in motion. In this case the figure is viewed from the side, so remember to consider which parts of the body will be seen.

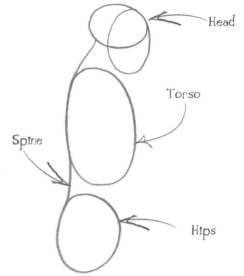

- Head
- Torso
- Spine
- Hips

Draw in the basic shapes for the head, torso and hips. Join these shapes with a line for the spine.

Add a small circle on the upper torso for the shoulders.

Add straight lines for the arms with small circles at the elbow joints.

Draw ovals to indicate the hands.

Draw a small circle in the middle of the hips. This indicates the top of each leg. Add straight lines for the legs with small circles for the knee joints.

Add in a basic triangular shape for each foot.

Using the construction lines as a guide, start to add the shape of the body.

Pay particular attention to the joints of each limb, drawing elbows and knees accordingly.

Use curved lines for the shape of the body.

You can often see mistakes in a drawing by looking at it in reverse in a mirror.

Start to add in the facial features.

Add in muscle structure.

Complete the details of the facial features and hair.

Add clothing to the figure.

Using the ovals as a guide, add detail to the hands.

Add tone for definition.

Add muscles to the legs using the joints as a guide.

Add shade to areas where light will not reach.

Add shoes.

Add socks.

Remove any unwanted construction lines.

49

Running figure

A running figure makes a dynamic and powerful action pose. Study the shapes made by someone running and then draw the basic structure. Try to get a strong sense of movement to give life to your drawing.

Draw in the basic shapes for the head, torso and hips. Add a line for the spine.

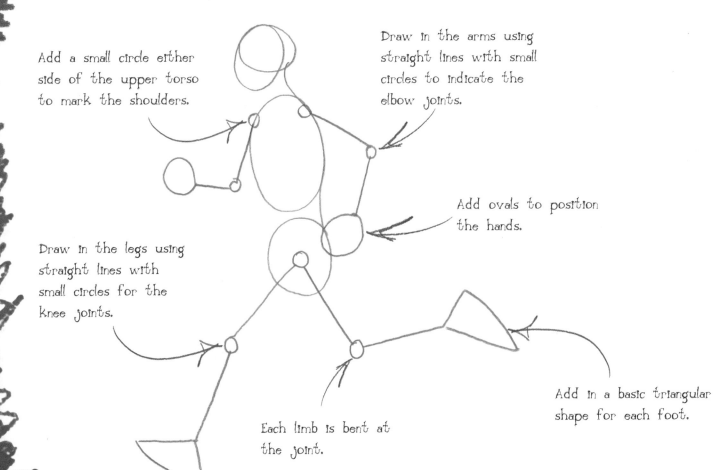

Add a small circle either side of the upper torso to mark the shoulders.

Draw in the arms using straight lines with small circles to indicate the elbow joints.

Add ovals to position the hands.

Draw in the legs using straight lines with small circles for the knee joints.

Each limb is bent at the joint.

Add in a basic triangular shape for each foot.

Add facial features to the head.

Sketch in the shape of the body. Use curved lines for arms and legs.

Add detail to the hands.

Proportions
Hold a pencil out at arm's length. Use it to help measure the proportions of the figure.

Draw in the shape of the trainers.

Complete the details of the facial features and the hair.

Add tone to define the muscles.

Add muscle to the arms and legs.

Draw in the clenched fists.

Add in clothing, making sure it fits around the body.

Add the detail of the trainers.

Add shade to areas where light would not reach.

Remove any unwanted construction lines.

51

Stick figures

^{DRAW}

Practise basic poses and quick stick figure drawings to get a sense of action into your basic poses. Getting the movement right in these early stages will make your completed drawing look better.

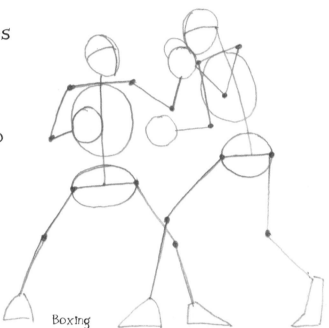

Boxing

Judo

Swordfight

Wrestling

Blocking a kick

High kick

Using construction lines from
the start of your drawing
helps you to create figures
with a more solid, 3-D feel.

Kendo

Ninja assassin

These stealthy warriors would attack under the cloak of darkness and were used by noblemen to assassinate their opponents.

Draw a curved line for the sword.

Add ovals for hands.

Draw in ovals for the head, body and hips. Add lines for the spine and hips.

Draw in lines for the legs with dots for joints.

Sketch in the arms with dots for joints.

Add basic shapes for the feet.

Composition

By framing your drawing with a square or a rectangle you can make it look completely different.

Draw a second curved line to create the shape of the sword.

Draw in the ninja's tunic, trousers, hood and facemask.

Position the eyes.

Add a belt.

Complete the sword details.

Add sleeves and hand guards.

Complete the facial features.

Draw in the ninja's long socks.

Leave some areas white to give the impression of folds in the fabric.

Add details to the traditional ninja footwear.

Add tone to areas where light would not reach.

Remove any unwanted construction lines.

55

DRAW Karate Kick

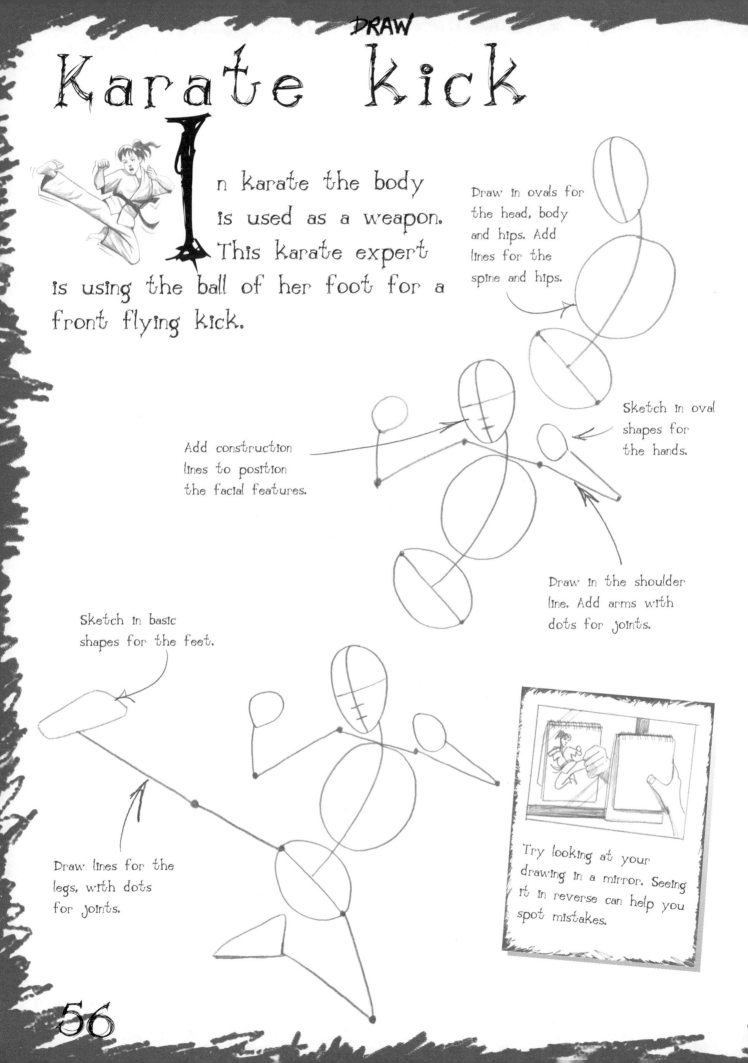

In karate the body is used as a weapon. This karate expert is using the ball of her foot for a front flying kick.

Draw in ovals for the head, body and hips. Add lines for the spine and hips.

Sketch in oval shapes for the hands.

Add construction lines to position the facial features.

Draw in the shoulder line. Add arms with dots for joints.

Sketch in basic shapes for the feet.

Draw lines for the legs, with dots for joints.

Try looking at your drawing in a mirror. Seeing it in reverse can help you spot mistakes.

Draw in facial features using the construction lines.

Draw the hair. The direction will emphasise movement.

Add toes and shape to the feet.

Add detail to the fists and forearms.

Position the belt.

Draw in the karategi trousers and tunic.

Add tone to the hair.

Complete all details of the feet.

Add tone and detail to the fists and forearms.

Finish off facial details.

Add dark tone to areas light wouldn't reach.

Complete the belt and add dark tone.

Add tone to show folds in the karategi.

Remove any unwanted construction lines.

Add movement lines.

57

Samurai DRAW battle

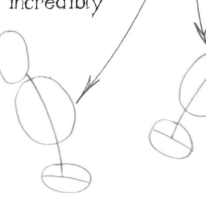

Samurai warriors fought in accordance with Japanese rules of honour and pride. They used a range of weapons which included incredibly sharp swords called katanas.

Draw in ovals for the heads, bodies and hips. Add lines for the spines and hips.

This samurai is seen in profile so the line of the spine is on the left hand side.

Add lines for the blade of each sword.

Add lines for the arms, with dots for the joints.

Sketch in ovals for the hands.

Add lines for the legs, with dots for the joints.

Draw in basic shapes for the feet.

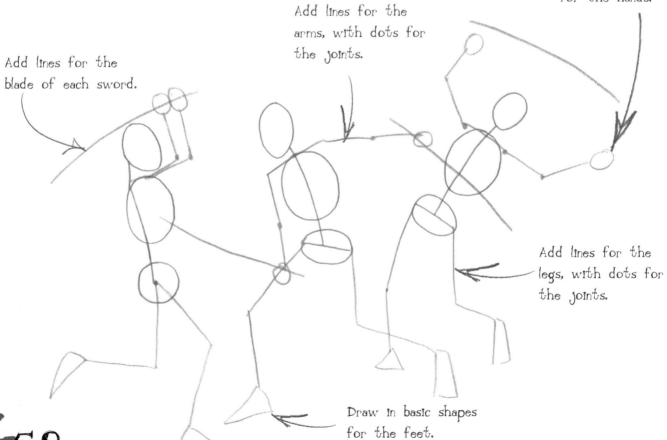

Add hair to each samurai.

Draw in the facial features.

Sketch in more shape to each sword.

Each samurai's robe is tied at the centre.

Using the construction lines as a guide, add the samurai's traditional clothing.

Finish off the facial details.

Add tone to areas where light wouldn't reach.

Add tone to the hair.

Add lines and tone to show folds in the fabric. Leave some areas white.

Complete the detail of the clothing by adding a pattern.

Finish the details of the feet.

Complete the details of each costume.

Remove any unwanted construction lines.

59

Armoured samurai

hese two heavily armoured samurai are from the Genpei War. The striking katana (samurai sword) is being blocked by the naginata (the staff).

Draw in ovals for the heads, bodies and hips. Add lines for the spines and hips.

Add lines for the arms, with dots for the joints.

Add a long line with a curved end for the naginata.

Draw in basic shapes for the helmets.

Add basic hand shapes.

Draw in basic shapes for the feet.

Draw in lines for the legs, with dots for the joints.

Complete the shape of the naginata.

Draw in fingers on each hand.

Add the complex decoration of the helmets.

Draw in the sleeves and wide samurai trousers.

Draw in the facial features.

Add the large plates of armour.

Sketch in the legs, indicating armour.

Add tone to areas light wouldn't reach.

Complete the samurai helmets and costume detail.

Add zig-zag details to the armour to show how it is made.

Finish the facial features.

Add tone to show shape and movement of trousers.

Complete the details of the naginata and katana.

Add armour to the legs and complete the feet.

Remove any unwanted construction lines.

61

Dramatic heights

The choice of background can often add tension and drama to extreme sports. Here are two sports seen from a great height. The use of perspective drawing in relation to the figure gives a great sense of height and danger.

The climber clings perilously to a rock face. Use perspective to show how steep the rockface is as it falls away into the distance.

Add shading to areas where the light wouldn't reach to help create a three-dimensional effect.

The parachutist falls to a faraway airfield.

Use perspective to draw in the airfield in relation to the falling parachutist.

Consider the scale of the buildings to show how far down the airfield is.

When your drawing is complete remove unwanted construction lines.

Freestyle BMX

The BMX is the perfect bike for freestyling. With pegs attached and a flexible setup, riders are capable of performing amazing tricks and stunts.

Start by drawing the rider as a simple stick figure with dots to indicate joints.

Add ovals for the head, body, hips and hands.

Using the construction lines as a guide add tube shapes for the legs and circles for knees.

Draw simple triangles for the feet.

Using straight lines mark out the frame of the BMX.

Sketch in the position of the facial features.

Using the construction lines as a guide, add tube shapes for the arms with circles for elbows.

Add more detail to the shape of the feet.

Add the BMX wheels to the bike frame.

Add parts of the frame and pegs.

Draw in the rider's T-shirt.

Add some hair and a cap.

Sketch in basic shapes for the hands and fingers.

Draw in the wheels using construction lines to help with perspective and scale.

Add shoes.

Sketch in the pedals.

Add the handle bars using the construction lines as a guide.

Add the main frame of the bike using straight lines.

Finish the detail of the head, hat and hair.

Add detail and creases to the trousers, especially behind the knee.

Add dark tone to areas where light would not reach.

Add detail to the shoes.

Finish the dark metal handlebars.

Finish the frame of the bike, adding a chain and details to the pedals. Add tone to suggest tubular metal.

Complete the wheels, adding dark tone for the rubber tyres and lines for the spokes.

Remove any unwanted construction lines.

DRAW Skysurfing

Skysurfing is a high-altitude extreme sport. A skysurfer freefalls from an aeroplane with a board attached to his feet, surfing the air and performing stunts on the way to the ground.

Start by sketching in a simple stick figure with dots for the joints.

Draw ovals for the head, body, hips and hands.

Draw in the shape of the hands.

Draw in simple tube shapes for the arms. Add circles for the elbows.

Position basic facial features and add a neck.

Connect the body and hip ovals together.

Sketch in tube shapes for the legs and attach them to the hip oval.

This arm and hand are shortened because of perspective.

Add circles for the knees.

Sketch in the board.

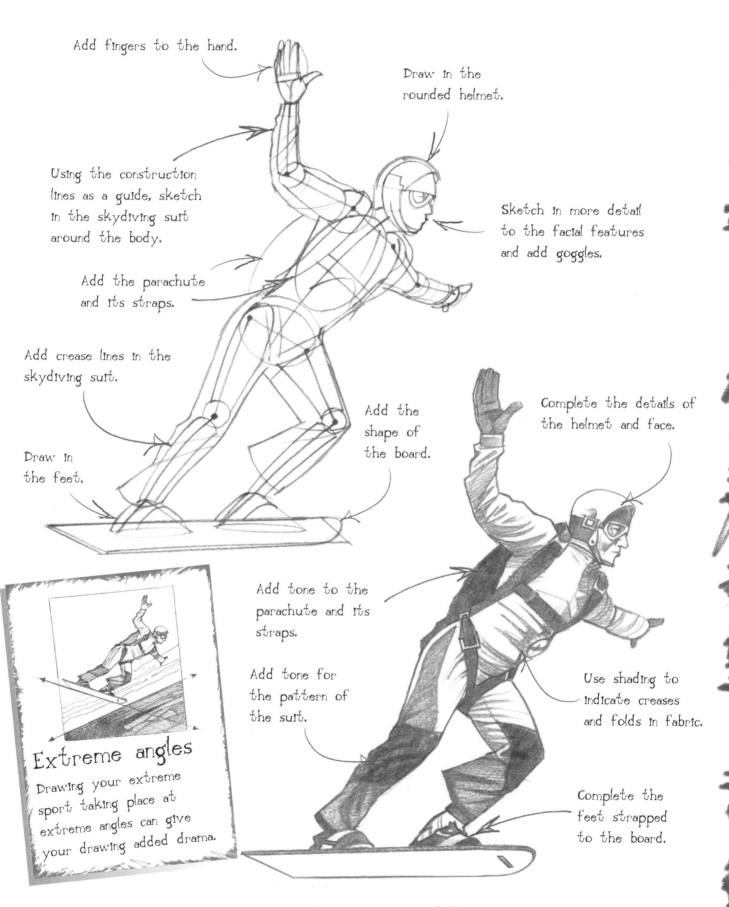

Add fingers to the hand.

Draw in the rounded helmet.

Using the construction lines as a guide, sketch in the skydiving suit around the body.

Sketch in more detail to the facial features and add goggles.

Add the parachute and its straps.

Add crease lines in the skydiving suit.

Complete the details of the helmet and face.

Draw in the feet.

Add the shape of the board.

Add tone to the parachute and its straps.

Use shading to indicate creases and folds in fabric.

Add tone for the pattern of the suit.

Extreme angles

Drawing your extreme sport taking place at extreme angles can give your drawing added drama.

Complete the feet strapped to the board.

Remove any unwanted construction lines.

67

Draw Wakeboarding

This extreme watersport involves being towed behind a boat at high speeds on a small wakeboard. Hitting the wake of the boat enables the wakeboarder to fly into the air and perform amazing tricks.

Draw ovals for the head, body and hands.

Add a line for the tow-rope handle.

Start by sketching in a simple stick figure with dots for the joints.

Add the shape of the feet.

Sketch in simple tube shapes for the arms.

Add some facial details.

Add circles for elbows.

Draw in the hand shapes.

Draw two parallel lines for the wakeboard.

Add more shape to the feet.

Draw in simple tube shapes for the legs, adding circles for knees.

Add curved windswept lines for hair.

Using the construction lines as a guide, add the curved shape of the arms.

Sketch in the tow rope.

Draw a vest on the figure.

Add fingers to the hands.

Draw a basic boot shape around the feet.

Add long baggy shorts.

Add tone to define muscle structure.

Finish the details of the tow rope and handle.

Complete the details of the head and hair.

Complete the shorts with a graphic design and creases.

Add folds and creases to the vest.

Finish the boot details.

Add the waves and splash of water.

Complete the wakeboard.

Remove any unwanted construction lines.

Skateboarding

DRAW

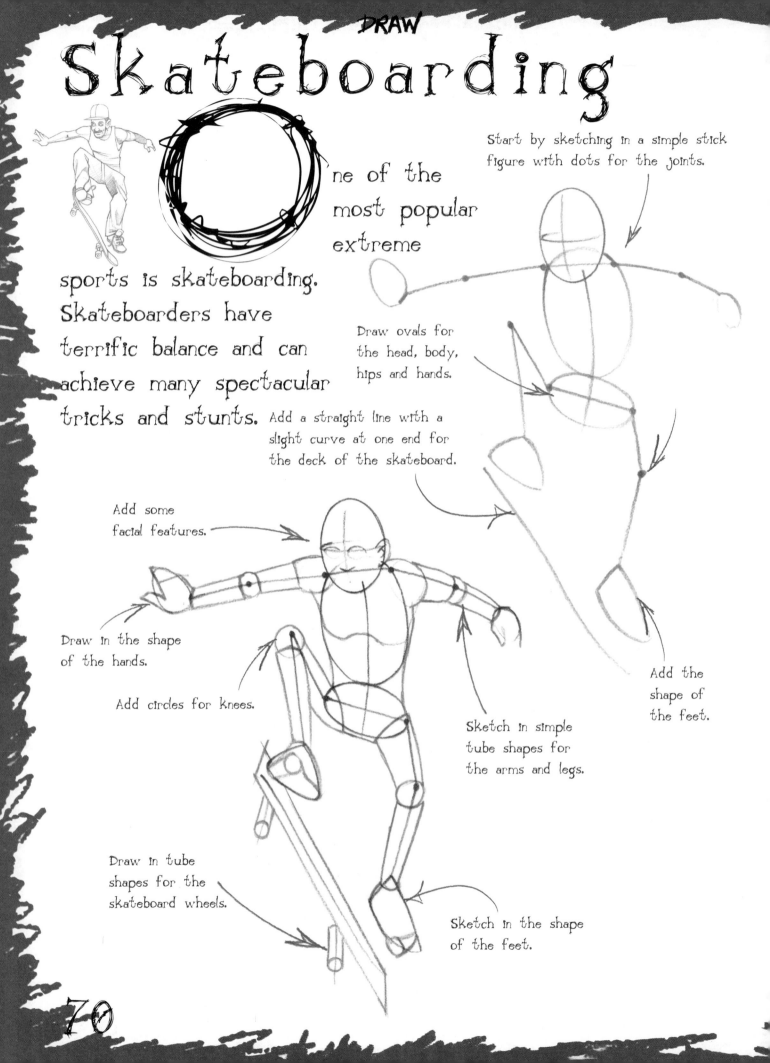

One of the most popular extreme sports is skateboarding. Skateboarders have terrific balance and can achieve many spectacular tricks and stunts.

Start by sketching in a simple stick figure with dots for the joints.

Draw ovals for the head, body, hips and hands.

Add a straight line with a slight curve at one end for the deck of the skateboard.

Add some facial features.

Draw in the shape of the hands.

Add circles for knees.

Sketch in simple tube shapes for the arms and legs.

Add the shape of the feet.

Draw in tube shapes for the skateboard wheels.

Sketch in the shape of the feet.

Add a cap to the head.

Draw in the fingers.

Draw in both arms using the construction lines as a guide. This arm is very foreshortened because of its angle.

Sketch in the trousers.

Add a vest.

Separate the tube into individual wheels.

Complete the facial details.

Add muscle detail to the arms.

Start to draw in the skaterboarder's shoes.

Add dark tone to areas where light would not reach.

Add creases to the trouser fabric.

Finish drawing the skateboard.

Shadows

Adding a shadow to your drawing can give it added drama. The shape of the skater's shadow will depend on the direction of the light source.

Finish drawing the skateboard shoes, adding laces and detail.

Remove any unwanted construction lines.

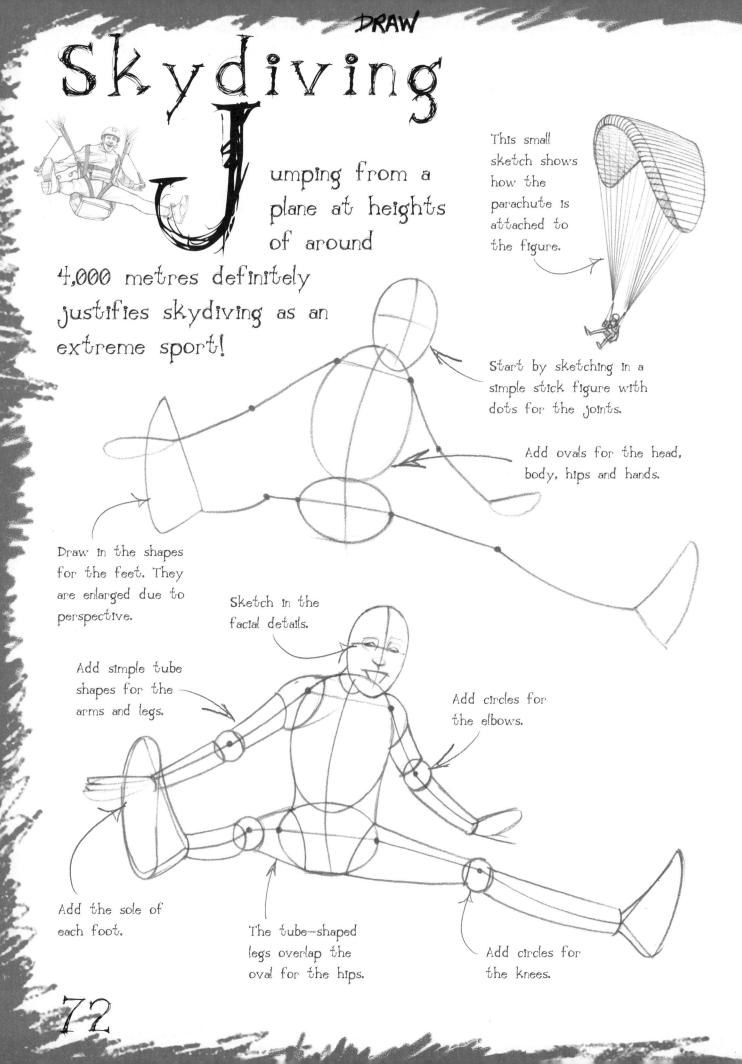

Skydiving

Jumping from a plane at heights of around 4,000 metres definitely justifies skydiving as an extreme sport!

This small sketch shows how the parachute is attached to the figure.

Start by sketching in a simple stick figure with dots for the joints.

Add ovals for the head, body, hips and hands.

Draw in the shapes for the feet. They are enlarged due to perspective.

Sketch in the facial details.

Add simple tube shapes for the arms and legs.

Add circles for the elbows.

Add the sole of each foot.

The tube-shaped legs overlap the oval for the hips.

Add circles for the knees.

72

Draw in the parachutist's jumpsuit.

Add a helmet.

Add all the parachute straps.

Sketch fingers onto the hands.

Sketch in the parachute toggles.

Add the shape of the shoes.

Add the shape of the parachute bag.

Add dark tone to all the straps of the parachute.

Complete the details of the face.

Add folds and creases to the jumpsuit.

Finish the boots.

Add tread to the sole of this shoe.

Complete the details of the parachute bag.

Remove any unwanted construction lines.

73

Action poses

DRAW

Motion and balance are important aspects to consider in your drawing. Use basic construction lines to create a variety of poses. Then build the drawing up from there.

Exaggerate the curve of the centre line to give movement and action to your figure.

Add shading to any areas where light would not reach.

Study real people to see how their bodies move.

Pay particular attention to the curve and direction of the spine and hips.

Use construction lines to make sure the balance of the fighting figures is accurate.

Use circle and oval shapes to position the joints.

Keep the drawing quite light and sketchy at first, until you are confident that the proportions are right.

75

Adding movement DRAW

The style and position of the movement lines that you draw can create many different types of fighting movement.

Start by sketching these simple shapes.

Head

Draw an oval for the head and body and smaller ovals for the hands.

Body

Sketch in the arms using straight lines. Add dots to indicate the joints.

Using your construction lines as a guide, sketch simple tube shapes for the arms.

Sketch in the positions of the facial features and hair.

Complete the facial features.

Add circles for the joints.

Add shading and tone to create muscle definition.

By changing the position and style of the movement lines, you can change the action of the figure.

Curved, sweeping lines create the effect of an arc-shaped punch.

Straight lines drawn in one direction give the impression of strong impact.

Faded movement lines create the effect that the hand is moving very fast.

DRAW
Jumping fighter

This character is launching himself off the ground and swinging a punch at the same time.

Start by sketching simple shapes for the figure.

Head

Body

Hips

Indicate the joints with dots.

Draw two lines to indicate the position and angle of the shoulders and hips. Draw a line for the spine.

Sketch in the positions of the facial features.

Using the construction lines as a guide, start drawing in the main shapes of the body.

Draw in tube shapes for the legs; note how the legs appear shorter as they angle towards or away from the viewer.

Add ovals for the feet.

78

Draw in the fingers in a clenched fist shape.

Add the outline of the clothing.

Add more detail to the face and sketch in the hair.

Add the curved structure of the upper body and indicate the position of the belt.

Add lines to indicate movement.

Complete the facial features.

Shade the bottom half of the leg.

Draw in the details of the clothing.

Complete the drawing of the boots.

Shade any areas where light would not reach.

Remember to remove any unwanted construction lines.

79

DRAW
Martial arts

Manga figures are often shown in action, performing martial arts moves.

Start by sketching these simple shapes for the figure.

Sketch an oval for the head.

Add an overlapping oval for the body and another for the hips.

Draw the limbs with straight lines.

Indicate the joints with dots.

Add circles for the joints.

Draw oval shapes to position the feet.

Sketch in the positions of the hands using curved shapes.

Sketch in the positions of the headband and nose.

Using your construction lines as a guide, sketch simple tube shapes for the arms and legs.

Draw in the shape of the fingers.

Manga characters generally have very stylised hair. Think about the situation and make the hair fit the scene.

Draw in the shape of the clothes, making sure that they go around the body and flare out at the ends of the limbs.

Add spiky hair and start to finish the face.

Draw the toes on the feet.

Add creases to the cloth.

Complete the facial features.

Add shading and tone to the clothes.

Remove any unwanted construction lines.

Complete the feet and ankles.

Action Kick
DRAW

This character is jumping in the air and doing a powerful high kick. The pose captures a sense of action and excitement.

Sketch in ovals for the head, body, hips, hands and feet.

Head

Body

Hips

Draw two lines to indicate the position and angle of the shoulders and hips.

Draw straight lines with dots at the joints for each of the limbs.

Fill out the arms and legs using simple tube shapes. The further arm looks small and the near leg very large because of the exaggerated perspective.

Indicate the position of the facial features.

Start to add the shape of the hands.

Add more detail to the shape of the feet.

Exaggerated features
Manga characters' facial features have a distinct style and shape. They often have oversized eyes which help when drawing expressions.

82

Add more detail to the facial features.

Draw in the shape of the fingers.

Finish drawing in the shape of the shoes.

Start drawing in the clothes. Make sure they curve around the body.

Draw in the clenched fist.

Draw straight lines coming from the kicking leg for added dramatic effect.

Finish drawing the detail of the hair and face.

Complete the detail of the clothing.

Add shading where light would not reach.

Add tone and creases to the clothing.

Remove any unwanted construction lines.

83

Falling in Fight

In battle it can be hard to keep your balance. This character is about to topple over and has a pained expression on his face.

Start by sketching these simple shapes for the figure.

Sketch an oval for the head.

Add an oval for the body and another for the hips.

Indicate the joints with dots.

Draw two lines to indicate the position and angle of the shoulders and hips. Draw in a curved line for the spine (see page 12).

Add fingers.

Sketch in the positions of the facial features.

Add circles for the joints.

Draw the limbs with straight lines.

Draw in the main shape of the body, using the ovals to guide you.

Draw triangle shapes to position the feet.

Using your construction lines as a guide, sketch the simple tube shapes for the arms and legs.

84

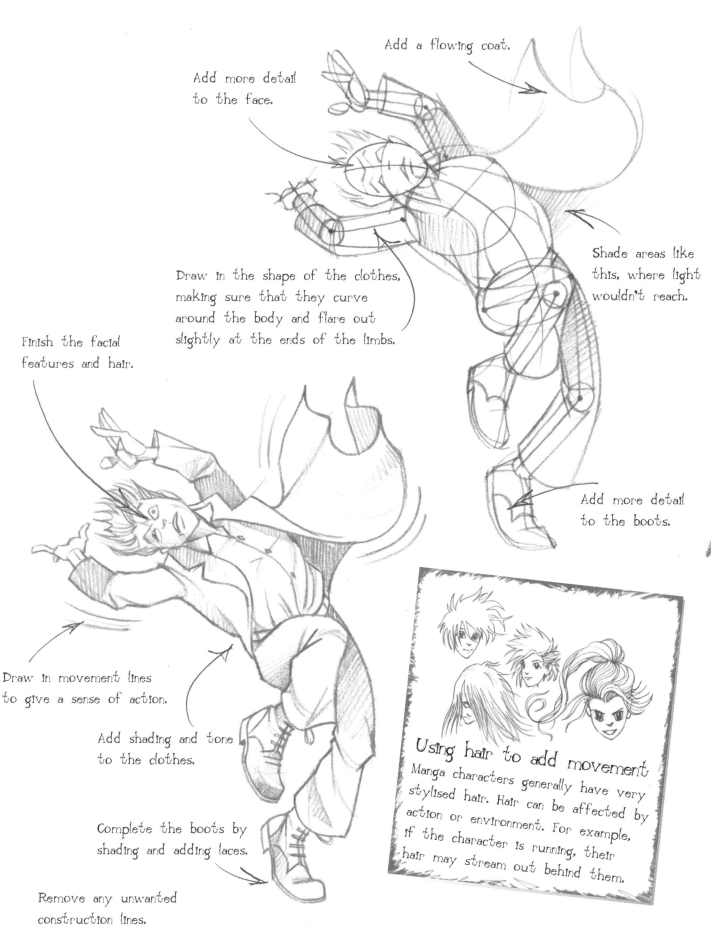

Add a flowing coat.

Add more detail to the face.

Shade areas like this, where light wouldn't reach.

Draw in the shape of the clothes, making sure that they curve around the body and flare out slightly at the ends of the limbs.

Finish the facial features and hair.

Add more detail to the boots.

Draw in movement lines to give a sense of action.

Add shading and tone to the clothes.

Complete the boots by shading and adding laces.

Remove any unwanted construction lines.

Using hair to add movement

Manga characters generally have very stylised hair. Hair can be affected by action or environment. For example, if the character is running, their hair may stream out behind them.

Heads

Heads come in many shapes and sizes, but this simple set of rules should help you draw any type.

First draw an oval (for a longer head and face, just make the oval longer and thinner).

Now add a narrower oval within the first. This is a construction line to show you where the centre line of the face is. The dotted part of this oval represents the back of the head.

Draw a third oval crossing the second one. This is another construction line to help you get the nose and eyes in the right place. Again, the dotted part shows the back of the head.

The point where the second and third ovals cross is the centre of the face. Draw in the eyes just above the centre.

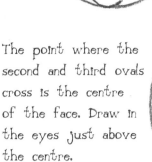

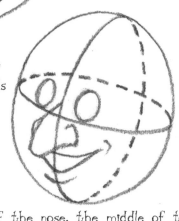

With these construction lines in place it is easier to place the facial features and draw the head.

The top of the nose, the middle of the mouth and the space between the eyes should all line up with the second oval.

You can make the head look in a different direction by changing the width of the inner ovals – this changes the position where the lines cross. This is very useful if you want to draw the same head from different angles.

Making the second oval wider makes the head face more to the side. The cross–over construction lines always help you to identify the centre of the face.

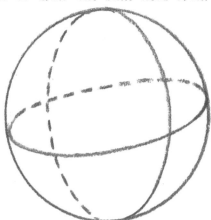
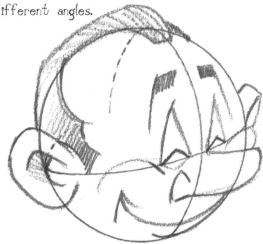

To draw a head facing downwards, the second and third ovals should cross in the lower half of the face. Use the construction lines each time to position the facial features. See how the mouth is mostly hidden by the nose.

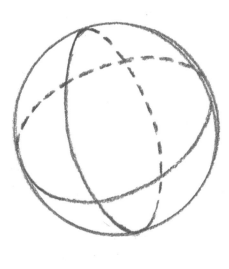

To make the head look upwards, the second and third ovals must cross in the upper half of the face. Again use the construction lines to draw in the features. See how much space the mouth takes up in this view.

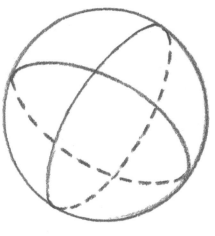

87

Expressions

Drawing different expressions is very important in cartoons. It's the best way to show what your character is thinking or feeling. Try drawing many different facial expressions. Don't be afraid to exaggerate them for comic effect.

Start by drawing an oval shape.

Head

Sketch in the other two ovals as you did before (pages 14—15).

Arched eyebrows.

Angular mouth

Using your construction lines as before, add the basic details of the face. This character looks angry.

Look at your own face in the mirror. By pulling different expressions, you will see how to draw these in your cartoons.

Gritted teeth

Finish the drawing by adding eyes, teeth and hair. Shade in the areas you want to be darker.

Now try drawing some different expressions. Here are a few ideas to get you started.

Giggling

Laughing

Frightened

Tired

Smiling

Puzzled

89

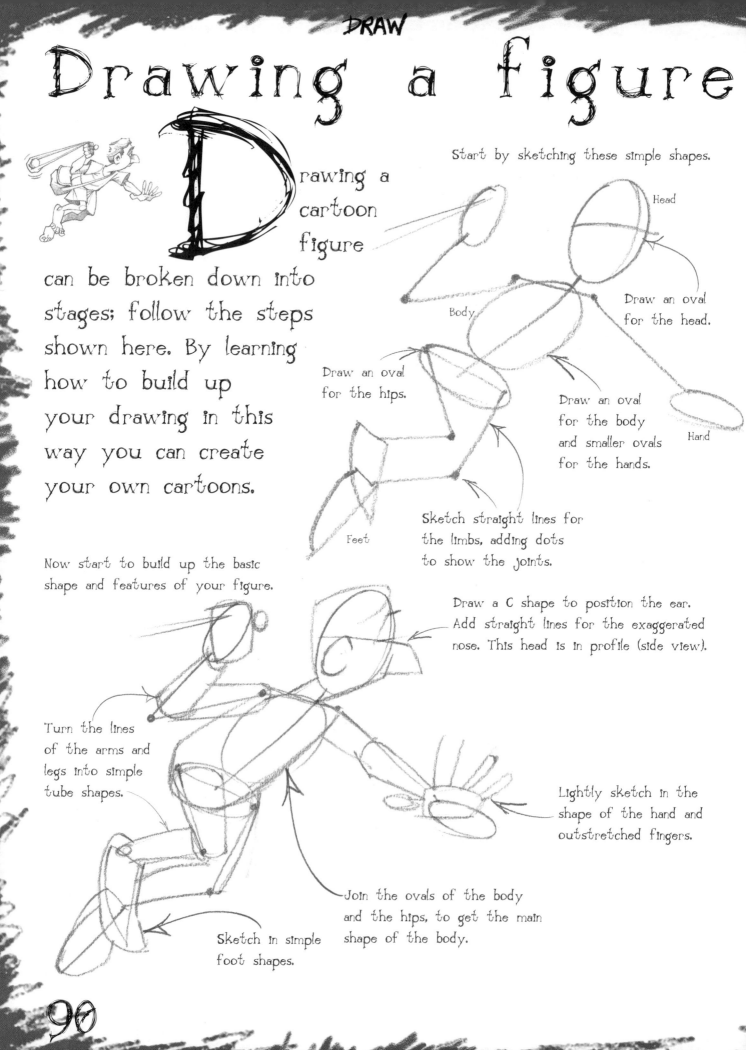

Drawing a figure

Drawing a cartoon figure can be broken down into stages; follow the steps shown here. By learning how to build up your drawing in this way you can create your own cartoons.

Start by sketching these simple shapes.

Head

Draw an oval for the head.

Body

Draw an oval for the body and smaller ovals for the hands.

Hand

Draw an oval for the hips.

Feet

Sketch straight lines for the limbs, adding dots to show the joints.

Now start to build up the basic shape and features of your figure.

Draw a C shape to position the ear. Add straight lines for the exaggerated nose. This head is in profile (side view).

Turn the lines of the arms and legs into simple tube shapes.

Lightly sketch in the shape of the hand and outstretched fingers.

Sketch in simple foot shapes.

Join the ovals of the body and the hips, to get the main shape of the body.

90

Now take your figure a stage further.

Add fingers to the clenched fist.

Using a series of simple lines, add details to the head, defining the shape of the nose, eye, ear and hair.

Add the slingshot and satchel.

Draw in the shape of the hand and its fingers.

Draw in the feet and toes.

Draw in the legs. You have already marked where the joints are.

Complete the slingshot, adding detail and shading.

Add shading to the head where necessary, and add lines to show the direction of the hair. Finish off the eyes with a dot for the pupil.

Curved lines like these around an object or figure can suggest movement.

Shade in areas where light wouldn't reach.

Draw in the tunic. Creases in the cloth help to show the direction of the arms and legs beneath.

Use shading on the palm of the hand, and add faint lines to show the joints in the fingers.

Complete any details of the feet and legs, adding toenails and kneecaps.

Carefully rub out any unwanted construction lines that remain.

91

Figure work

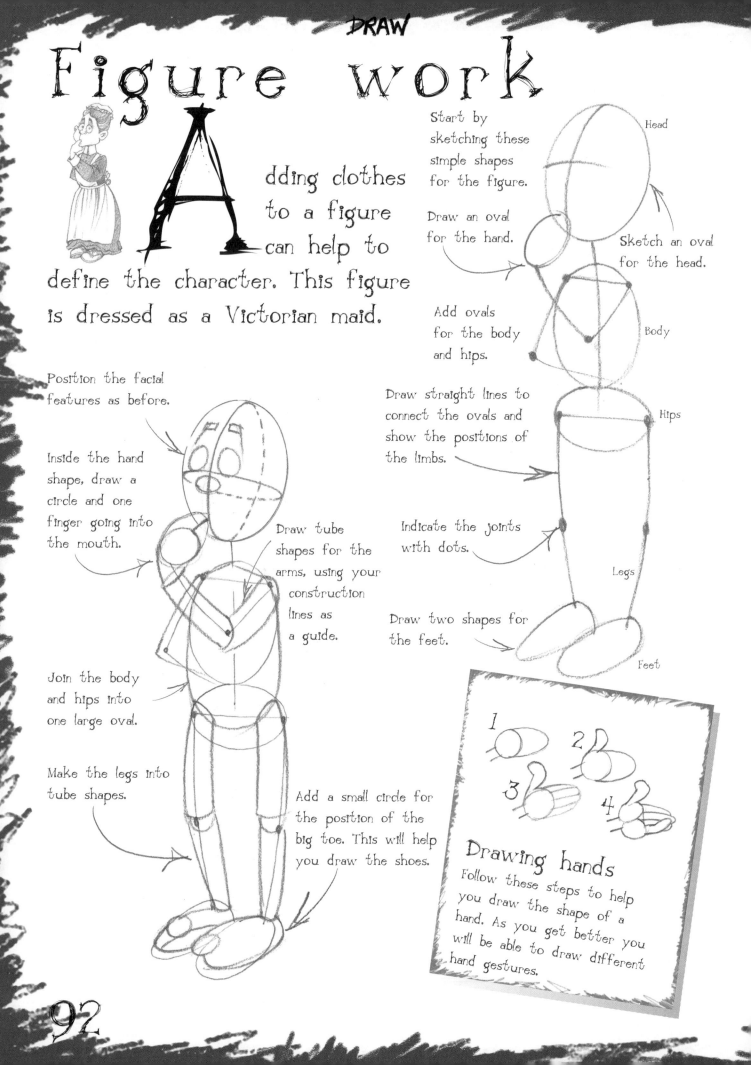

Adding clothes to a figure can help to define the character. This figure is dressed as a Victorian maid.

Start by sketching these simple shapes for the figure.

Draw an oval for the hand.

Head

Sketch an oval for the head.

Add ovals for the body and hips.

Body

Draw straight lines to connect the ovals and show the positions of the limbs.

Hips

Indicate the joints with dots.

Legs

Position the facial features as before.

Inside the hand shape, draw a circle and one finger going into the mouth.

Draw tube shapes for the arms, using your construction lines as a guide.

Draw two shapes for the feet.

Feet

Join the body and hips into one large oval.

Make the legs into tube shapes.

Add a small circle for the position of the big toe. This will help you draw the shoes.

Drawing hands

Follow these steps to help you draw the shape of a hand. As you get better you will be able to draw different hand gestures.

Add more facial features and draw in the shape of the face, using the construction lines as a guide.

Sketch in the hair and add the cap.

Draw the shape of the clothes going around the body.

Sketch in the dress using curved lines.

Dress

Add details such as cuffs, buttons and a collar.

Finish the head by adding the hair and eyelashes. Shade above the eyes and inside the ear.

Add lines to the apron and at the bottom of the dress to show folds in the material.

The hem of the dress covers part of the feet.

Two parallel lines show the soles of the shoes.

Try drawing these hand gestures.

Add shading to areas like this where light wouldn't reach.

Remove any unwanted construction lines.

Glossary

Chiaroscuro The practice of drawing high-contrast pictures with a lot of black and white, but not much grey.

Composition The arrangement of the parts of a picture on the drawing paper.

Construction lines Guidelines used in the early stages of a drawing. They are usually erased later.

Fixative A type of resin used to spray over a finished drawing to prevent smudging. **It should only be used by an adult.**

Focal point A central point of interest.

Foreshortening Drawing part of a figure shorter than it really is, so it looks as though it is pointing towards the viewer.

Light source The direction from which the light seems to come in a drawing.

Perspective A method of drawing in which near objects are shown larger than faraway objects to give an impression of depth.

Pose The position assumed by a figure.

Proportion The correct relationship of scale between each part of the drawing.

Silhouette A drawing that shows only a flat, dark shape, like a shadow.

Three-dimensional Having an effect of depth, so as to look lifelike or real.

Vanishing point The place in a perspective drawing where parallel lines appear to meet.

Index